Bugs in the

David Bauer

Illustrated by Burgandy Beam

M000033040

Rigby®

A Harcourt Achieve Imprint

www.Rigby.com
1-800-531-5015

I see a bug!
This bug is black.

3

I see a bug!
This bug is orange.

5

I see a bug!
This bug is green.

I see a bug!
This bug is brown.

I see a bug!
This bug is yellow.

I see a bug!
This bug is purple.

I see a bug!
This bug is red.

Bugs are fun!